FLIGHT

AIRPLANES

June Loves

This edition first published in 2002 in the United States of America by Chelsea House
Publishers, a subsidiary of Haights Cross Communications

Chelsea House Publishers
1974 Sproul Road, Suite 400
Broomall, PA 19008-0914

The Chelsea House world wide web address is www.chelseahouse.com

Library of Congress Cataloging-in-Publication Data Applied for.
ISBN 0-7910-6560-X

First Published in 2000 by
Macmillan Education Australia Pty Ltd
627 Chapel Street, South Yarra, Australia, 3141

Text copyright © June Loves 2000

Edited by Lara Whitehead
Text design by if Design
Cover design by if Design
Page layout by if Design / Raul Diche
Illustrations by Lorenzo Lucia
Printed in Hong Kong

Acknowledgements
The author and the publisher are grateful to the following for permission to reproduce
copyright material:

Cover: sea plane (center), courtesy of Coo-ee Picture Library; concorde (background),
Ruth Lathlean/World Images.

Photographs courtesy of: Coo-ee Historical Picture Library, pp. 2 (right), 4 (left), 4–5, 6–7,
7 (top and middle right), 8, 10, 11, 12–3, 14, 15, 22; Coo-ee Picture Library, pp. 3 (right),
23, 24–5, 26–7 (top), 27 (right); Great Southern Stock, pp. 19, 26 (bottom); Lochman
Transparencies, p. 17; Ruth Lathlean/World Images, pp. 2–3 (background), 28 (top right),
29, 30–1, 32.

While every care has been taken to trace and acknowledge copyright the publishers
tender their apologies for any accidental infringement where copyright has proved
untraceable.

Contents

Early airplanes

SINCE VERY EARLY TIMES, people have dreamed of flying like the birds. There are many myths, legends and ancient stories about people's attempts to fly. The ancient Greek myth of Daedalus and his son Icarus is one.

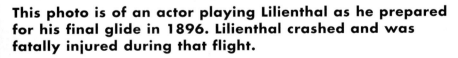

This photo is of an actor playing Lilienthal as he prepared for his final glide in 1896. Lilienthal crashed and was fatally injured during that flight.

GLIDERS

During the 1800s, German engineer Otto Lilienthal (1848-96) designed, built and flew **gliders**, which are airplanes without engines. He and others provided inspiration and successful flying models for future inventors and pilots. Between 1893 and 1896, Lilienthal made about 2,500 successful glides, mostly in **monoplane** hang-gliders in which he flew distances of up to 300 meters (984 feet).

Building and testing gliders

The early gliders led the way for the development of the airplane. The Wright brothers were admirers of Otto Lilienthal and the American engineer Otto Chanute. Wilbur and Orville Wright read about their experiments with gliders and followed their progress.

Before they actually designed and flew their first airplane, the Wright brothers spent many years of hard work designing, building and experimenting with gliders. They tested various glider designs, flying them like kites before they flew in the gliders themselves.

The '1902 Glider'

The '1902 Glider' built by the Wright brothers was a double-winged or **biplane** design. The pilot lay in the middle on his stomach and operated the **rudder** and **elevator**, which was like a tail plane on the front of the plane. To control the plane, the pilot operated the front elevator with his hands and the **wing-warp** mechanism by a bar at his feet.

The '1902 Glider' had a wooden frame and cotton covering.

Flying Fact

Sir George Cayley built and flew the first successful model glider in 1804.

The first flight

IN 1903, THE FIRST powered flight took place, beginning the age of air transportation as we know it. On December 17, 1903, the first airplane, the Flyer, took to the air at Kitty Hawk in North Carolina, USA. It was invented and built by the Wright brothers and piloted by Orville Wright. This was the first controlled sustained flight by a heavier-than-air aircraft. The Flyer's first flight covered 36 meters (118 feet) at a height of about three meters (10 feet) and it stayed in the air for 12 seconds. The Wright brothers made three more flights on the same day.

 Flying Fact

The Wright brothers tested their airplanes at a remote and isolated beach called Kitty Hawk. Kitty Hawk beach had strong, reliable winds to help the airplanes get airborne.

Orville Wright making the first flight at Kitty Hawk, 1903.

Pioneer aviators

Orville Wright

THE WRIGHT BROTHERS

The Wright brothers, Wilbur (1867-1912) and Orville (1871-1948), worked closely together to invent, build and fly the first airplanes.

Early life

During their childhood, the Wright brothers were interested in mechanical things. They started a printing business and published daily newspapers. They also set up The Wright Cycle Company where they repaired, rented and designed bicycles. The success of The Wright Cycle Company helped support them as they developed the first airplanes.

Military contract

In the beginning, people thought of the Wright brothers' early flights as a novelty. This soon changed, however. In 1908, Orville Wright demonstrated a more powerful version of the Flyer to the American War Department. In 1909, the Wright brothers obtained the first contract to build planes for the military.

Wilbur Wright

The Flyer

THE WRIGHT BROTHERS designed the flyer to carry a single person. The pilot lay across the middle of the lower wing. He moved his body from side to side to control the plane in banking (turning) **maneuvers**. A cradle around the pilot's hips was attached by wires and pulleys to the wing tips. When the pilot moved his hips he could twist one wing tip or the other to maintain balance in flight.

The Wright brothers' patented airplane.

ELEVATORS

To make the Flyer go up or down, the Wright brothers used an elevator, or horizontal rudder. On Wright aircraft, the elevators were at the front. On most aircraft today they are at the rear.

WING SHAPE

The Wright brothers knew that aircraft wings had to be curved rather than flat. The Flyer's wings measured 12.29 meters (40 feet) from tip to tip. They were wooden frames covered with a cotton fabric.

THE FLYER'S ENGINE

The Wright brothers designed and built their own lightweight, four-cylinder gasoline engine. It produced about 15 **horsepower**. They used bicycle chains to transfer power to the propeller.

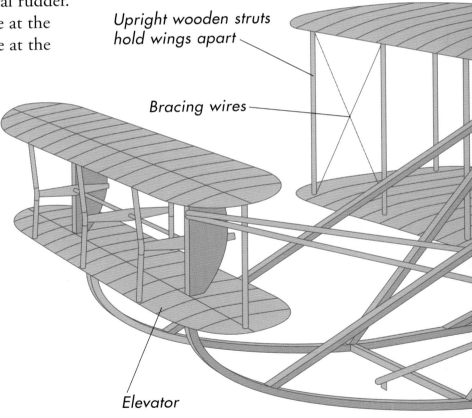

Upright wooden struts hold wings apart

Bracing wires

Elevator

The Flyer.

BANKING

The Wright brothers observed and noted how birds twisted or warped their wings to turn and maneuver in the air. This helped them with their wing designs so that the aircraft could bank (turn) in the air.

SPARS

A spar is the long rod inside an airplane's wing that gives it strength and stiffness. One or more spars usually run from the wing root near the **fuselage** out to the wing tip. The Flyer had two main spars in each wing. They were made of light, strong spruce wood.

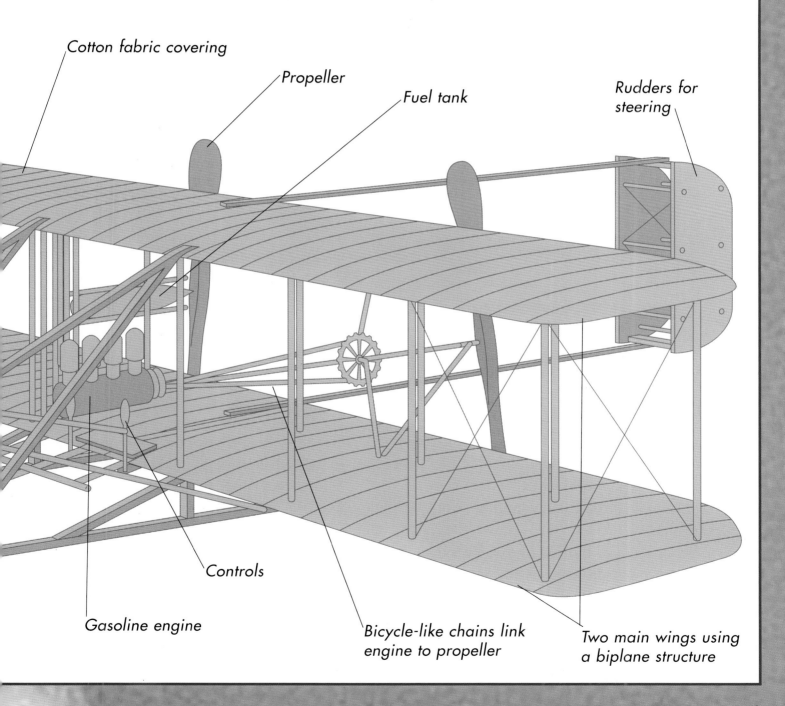

Cotton fabric covering

Propeller

Fuel tank

Rudders for steering

Controls

Gasoline engine

Bicycle-like chains link engine to propeller

Two main wings using a biplane structure

Developing better airplanes

AFTER THE EARLY flights of the Flyer, the Wright brothers continued to build better airplanes. They kept experimenting and testing to develop safer and more reliable aircraft.

Following the Wright brothers success, pilots and inventors also worked to improve airplanes. Almost every year airplanes flew faster and further than they had flown the year before.

Cockpits in the early planes had few instruments. To navigate, pilots used maps and flew straight toward landmarks.

EARLY AIRPLANE DESIGNS

The early years of airplanes were a time of great experimentation. Many different airplanes were designed, built and tested. There were no rules or standards to follow when building the early airplanes.

Airplanes were built with one, two or three or more sets of wings. Monoplanes had longer, weaker, single wings. Biplanes had two shorter, stronger wings. Biplanes were very popular as fighter planes in World War I, which lasted from 1914 to 1918.

FLYING EARLY AIRPLANES

The early planes were difficult and dangerous to fly and there were many accidents. Engine failures and other problems were common with the early airplanes. Forced landings, when pilots had to land their airplanes as quickly as possible in an emergency, happened often. Pilots often risked imprisonment if they landed in foreign countries without permission.

Air races and competitions

IN THE 1920S AND 1930S airplanes became safer and more reliable. This spurred many competitions and air races to see which planes were the fastest. Many prizes were offered to pilots looking for challenges. These air races and competitions encouraged improvement in airplane design.

FLYING RECORDS

The early aviators often designed, built and flew their own airplanes. In the 1920s and 1930s, daring pioneer aviators set records for distance and speed flying. To make or break a flying record, flights were classified by the type of aircraft, the speed, the distance and the altitude.

The first international flight

On July 25, 1909, the famous French aviator Louis Bleriot (1872-1936) won a prize of 1,000 pounds sterling (US$1,430) offered by the London Daily Mail newspaper for being the first aviator to fly across the English Channel. He flew across the Channel in a monoplane he had designed and built.

CASH PRIZES

Cash prizes were offered to aviators for long-distance flights to all parts of the world. Governments and business people wanted to establish air routes for commercial airlines to carry passengers and mail.

Thirty-five minutes after leaving Calais, France, Louis Bleriot landed in Dover, England, to a hero's welcome. His flight proved that people could fly long distances and land safely.

LONG DISTANCE FLIGHTS

The routes from England to Australia and between Europe and America became tests of endurance for pilots and their airplanes. The pioneer aviators had to be physically fit to fly the many hours required for long-distance flying.

Many hours of planning and preparation were needed for these flights. The pioneer aviators needed excellent navigational skills. Navigation over the wide expanses of sea was a hit-and-miss affair because there were often no maps available for the area they were flying in.

 Flying Fact

Charles Lindbergh flew the Spirit of St. Louis non-stop from New York to Paris at an average speed of 173 kilometers (107 miles) per hour, sometimes as high as 3,000 meters (9,843 feet) above the ocean.

RECORD-BREAKING FLIGHTS

John Alcock and Arthur Whitten Brown were famous British aviators. In June, 1919, they flew the first non-stop flight across the Atlantic Ocean. Their plane flew from Newfoundland, Canada to Ireland, a journey of 3,032 kilometers (1,884 miles), in 16 hours and 27 minutes. Their airplane, a Vickers Vimy bomber, became stuck in a bog on arriving in Ireland.

In 1919, after Alcock and Whitten Brown's first flight across the Atlantic Ocean, a prize of $25,000 was offered for the first successful flight in either direction between the United States and France. This was almost twice as far as the distance flown by Alcock and Whitten Brown. It was not until 1927 that the prize was claimed by Charles Lindbergh.

Charles Lindbergh landing the Spirit of St. Louis in Paris 1927.

The first solo flight across the Atlantic Ocean

Charles Lindbergh made the first solo flight across the Atlantic Ocean from New York to Le Bourget Airport, Paris, in May, 1927. He covered the distance of 5,810 kilometers (3,610 miles) in 33 1/2 hours through fog, rain and storms. His single-engine Ryan aircraft was named the Spirit of St. Louis.

It was a very dangerous journey for one man without a co-pilot. Lindbergh could not fall asleep or lose concentration for one second. He took only homemade sandwiches to eat. People gave him a hero's welcome when he returned to the United States.

PROBLEMS FOR EARLY AVIATORS

* Poor vision—from sun, sand, wind, hail or ice.
* Blisters and cold—from sunburn, engine heat and flying at high altitudes.
* Cramp and damp—from sitting in small, open cockpits.
* Deafness and dizziness—from loud engines and long hours in flight.
* Poisoning—from **carbon monoxide** exhaust from the engines.
* Lack of space—for food and essential supplies such as a parachute.
* Bad weather—fog and storms.
* Unreliable engines—often caused dangerous forced landings.
* Difficult landings—landing on bumpy ground, in mountainous areas or in bad conditions.

The first woman to fly solo from England to Australia

In May, 1930, Englishwoman Amy Johnson won a prize of 10,000 pounds sterling (US$14,300) when she landed in Darwin in her De Havilland Gypsy Moth biplane.

The Daily Mail, a British newspaper, had offered the prize for the first woman to fly the solo trip on the England-to-Australia run. She completed the journey in 19 1/2 days. During the flight, she also set the record for the fastest time from London to India, taking just six days to cover the distance.

In her cockpit, Amy Johnson carried tools, spare parts, tires, inner tubes, clothes, a sun helmet, mosquito netting, a first aid kit and a long knife for sharks.

The first flight across the Pacific Ocean

In 1928, Charles Kingsford-Smith and Charles Ulm made the first flight across the Pacific Ocean in a three-engine Fokker aircraft, the Southern Cross, which had earlier been used for exploring the North Pole. The monoplane was modified to take extra engines and fuel tanks that were needed for the long journey across the sea. Charles Kingsford-Smith and Charles Ulm received a gift of 5,000 pounds (US$7,150) from the Australian government.

Amy Johnson in her Gypsy Moth, 1930.

Bert Hinkler was a famous Australian aviator. In 1928, he broke several records in his airplane, an Avro Avian.

- ✶ The first non-stop flight from London to Rome.
- ✶ The fastest flight from England to India.
- ✶ The fastest flight from England to Australia.
- ✶ The first solo flight from England to Australia in less than 16 days.
- ✶ The longest plane flight.
- ✶ The longest solo flight that took less than 16 days.

Flying Fact

At the 1909 air show, the French pilot Hubert Latham won a prize when he flew his plane, the Antoinette, to a height of 155 meters (508 feet).

The first flights over the South Pole and the North Pole

Commander Richard Byrd (1888-1957) was a famous American explorer and aviator. In November, 1919, he and his crew became the first people to fly over the South Pole in a Ford 4-AT tri-motor airplane. Then, in May, 1926, Byrd and his crew became the first to fly over the North Pole. They flew their three-engine Fokker airplane.

The first solo flight across the Atlantic Ocean by a woman

In 1932, Amelia Earhart (1897-1937) flew solo across the Atlantic from Harbour Grace, Newfoundland, Canada to Culmore, Ireland. The flight lasted over 15 hours. Amelia Earhart became a popular heroine because of her courage and skill and received many awards.

Amelia Earhart in 1921.

Amelia Earhart was the first woman to accomplish many flying feats.

* ☆ Fly solo across the Atlantic Ocean.
* ☆ Receive the Distinguished Flying Cross.
* ☆ Fly from Honolulu to the mainland of the United States.
* ☆ Fly across the United States solo in both directions.

Light aircraft

SMALL, LIGHT AIRPLANES are usually called light aircraft. They have one or two engines that drive propellers. Most light airplanes are monoplanes, which means they have one set of wings.

Light airplanes do not need large airports to take off and land as larger planes do. These small planes are used to carry passengers and goods to remote places. They are also used to train pilots and for hobby and leisure flying.

PARTS OF A SMALL AIRCRAFT

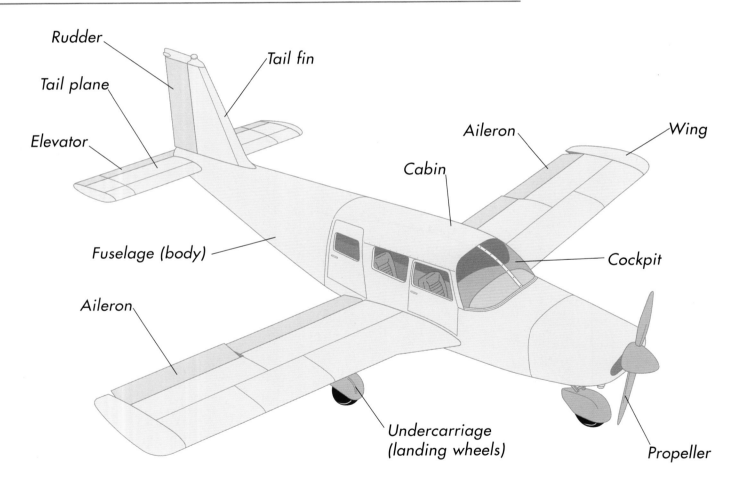

Rudder

Tail fin

Tail plane

Elevator

Aileron

Wing

Cabin

Fuselage (body)

Cockpit

Aileron

Undercarriage (landing wheels)

Propeller

AILERONS, ELEVATORS AND RUDDER

The **ailerons**, elevators and rudder are hinged control surfaces on the tail and the wings of an airplane. They are used to steer the airplane from left to right, as well as up and down.

How an airplane flies

FOUR FORCES ACT on an airplane when it is flying.

Lift is an upward force that holds an airplane in the air.

Thrust is the force that moves the airplane forward.

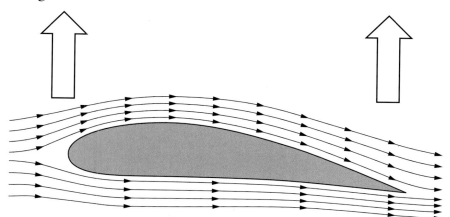

Drag is air resistance that holds the airplane back.

Weight is the force that pulls the airplane down.

An airplane's wings

The wings of an airplane are a special shape, called an **airfoil**. The top of the wing is curved and the bottom of the wing is straight.

Lift comes from an airplane's wings. Because the top of the wing is curved, air has further to go over the top than it does under the wing. This produces a lifting pressure over the wings that supports the weight of the airplane.

Flying Fact

An airplane can go up and down, turn sideways and roll over.

All airplanes have wings. The shape of the wings depends on how fast and high an airplane is designed to fly.

CONTROLLING AN AIRPLANE

To steer an airplane, pilots have to move two sets of controls in the cockpit, the control column with their hands and the rudder pedals with their feet. They move control surfaces on the airplane's wings and tail. These control surfaces alter the air pressures acting on the airplane's wings and tail, and allow the pilot to steer the airplane in any direction.

Rolling
The ailerons are raised on one wing and lowered on the other to roll the aircraft.

Yawing
When the rudder is moved from one side to the other, the aircraft's nose moves left or right.

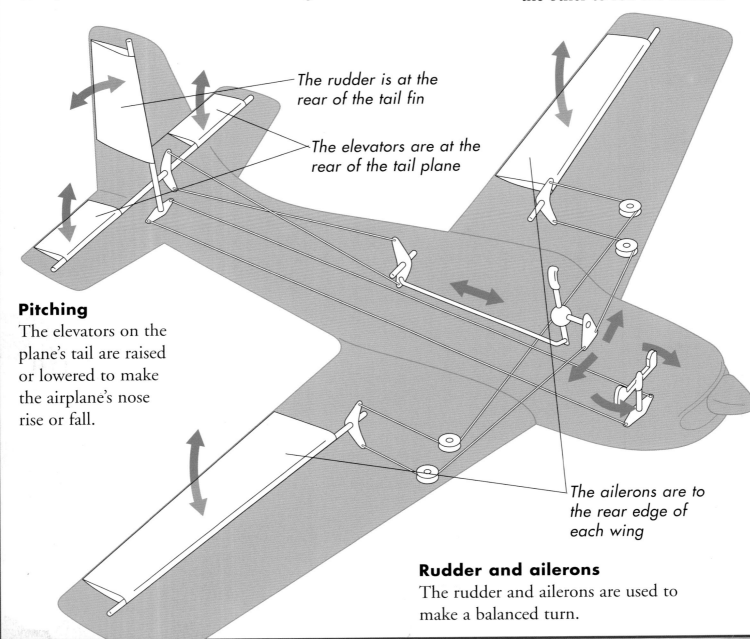

The rudder is at the rear of the tail fin

The elevators are at the rear of the tail plane

Pitching
The elevators on the plane's tail are raised or lowered to make the airplane's nose rise or fall.

The ailerons are to the rear edge of each wing

Rudder and ailerons
The rudder and ailerons are used to make a balanced turn.

AIRPLANE INSTRUMENTS

Four main airplane instruments help pilots tell how fast the aircraft is moving, how high above the ground it is, which direction it is headed and which way is up.

Autopilot systems

Many aircraft use computer-controlled autopilot systems. Modern autopilots can be used for take-off and landing, as well as for cruising. Frequent computer checks are made by pilots to make sure that every part of the airplane is working correctly.

An altimeter measures height above the ground

An airspeed indicator measures speed through the air

An attitude indicator shows whether the aircraft is flying with its wings level, nose up or nose down

A compass shows the direction the airplane is flying

PROPELLERS AND PISTONS

Propellers are driven by the airplane's engines. As a propeller turns, its blades force air backward at a much higher speed. This propels the airplane forward.

The first airplanes were powered by piston engines that turned propellers. Many airplanes are still powered this way today.

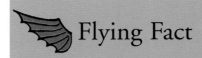

Flying Fact

In early airplanes, the propellers had to be spun by hand to start the engine. Until the 1940s, most propellers were made of wood.

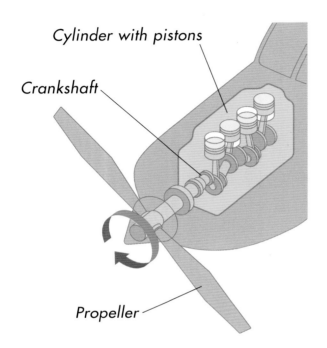

Cylinder with pistons

Crankshaft

Propeller

How an airplane's piston engine works

An airplane's piston engine is similar to a car engine. Inside the engine, the cylinders contain pistons. A mixture of fuel and air is burnt rapidly to drive the pistons. The pistons then push the **crankshaft** around. The crankshaft rotates and turns the propeller.

How a propeller works

A propeller accelerates a large mass of air to a higher speed. It draws air in the front, accelerates it, and throws it backward. By doing this continuously, the propeller produces a continuous forward thrust.

Airfoil shape

Propellers have an airfoil shape. The front of each blade is curved more than the back. As the blades spin, the air pressure is lower in front of them than behind. The difference in air pressure pulls the aircraft forward.

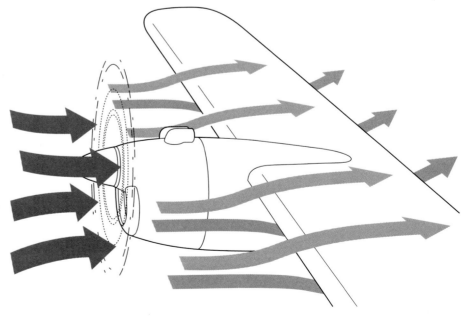

Jet engines

JET ENGINES CAN PROPEL airplanes to greater speeds than piston engines. Most airliners, military airplanes and many small business airplanes are powered by jet engines. There are three main types of jet engines: turbojet, turboprop and turbofan.

TURBOJET ENGINES

Turbojet engines are an earlier type of jet engine. They are noisier than turbofan engines and use more fuel.

TURBOPROP ENGINES

Turboprop engines work like turbojets but drive a propeller, which produces most of the thrust. They use less fuel but are slower than turbojet or turbofan engines and are used on slower aircraft.

TURBOFAN ENGINES

Today most big airliners are powered by turbofan engines. They are quieter and cooler than other jet engines. Turbofans suck air in and force it out at the back at great speed. This thrusts the aircraft in the opposite direction.

How a turbofan engine works

1 Compressor blades compress the air as it flows through.
2 Burning fuel heats the air in the combustion chamber, which causes the air to expand rapidly.
3 The hot gas turns the turbine. The turbine drives the fan and compressor blades.
4 Fan air and hot gas are expelled at high speed from the back.

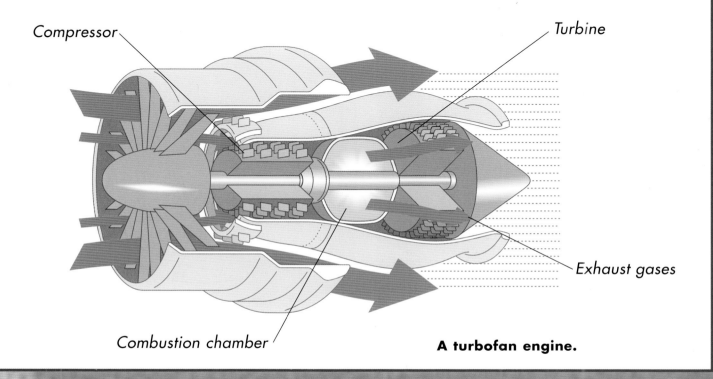

Compressor

Turbine

Exhaust gases

Combustion chamber

A turbofan engine.

Early airliners

THE FIRST AIRLINERS

Commercial air travel began after World War I. The first airliners were converted from World War I bombers. A passenger terminal and a grass field were all most early airliners needed because they were not heavy enough to require concrete runways.

The early passenger planes were small, noisy, and slow. Flights were sometimes very bumpy and were often cancelled because of bad weather.

The first airliners only took a small number of passengers. Passengers were fitted out with coats, goggles and often hot-water bottles because it was very cold travelling in the cockpit or cabin. Even though it was uncomfortable, many rich people wanted to use this new, exciting way of travel.

Airliners designed especially to carry passengers were built from the 1920s. An important advance in the 1930s was the development of all-metal fuselages and wings. This gave the airliners great streamlined shape and space and comfort for passengers.

AIRSHIPS

The giant Zeppelin airships were competing with airliners at this time by offering a first-class, long-distance passenger service. When the Hindenberg was destroyed by fire in 1937, killing 36 people on board, people lost confidence in airships as a means of air travel.

Handle Page HP42

The HP42 airliner series, which were converted bombers with a biplane design, were early airliners famous for their reliability and safety. They were run by Imperial Airways and set new standards of luxury for passengers in the 1930s.

Early biplanes offered few comforts for the passengers.

The Douglas DC-2 and DC-3

The best airliner of the mid-1930s was the Douglas DC-2. It had a retractable undercarriage and streamlined design. An even better successor followed soon after, called the DC-3. Some of these planes are still flying today.

Pressurised cabins

Pressurized cabins allow passengers and crew to breathe as though they were at a lower altitude. This enables airliners to fly above the weather. All-metal airliners with pressurized cabins were carrying passengers by 1939.

The first version of the Lockheed Constellation flew in 1943. It was the world's heaviest and fastest airliner at the time. It began a regular passenger service from New York to Paris in 1945. The journey took 13 hours

A DC-3.

23

Modern airliners

TODAY, THE MODERN AIRLINER is the fastest way to travel. Airliners can range in size from small propeller-driven planes used for short journeys to jumbo jets that fly enormous distances.

Airliners have become much faster and larger since the first passenger services began. There are more than 500 airline companies in the world, each with its own markings on the body and tail of the airliner.

Today's jumbo jets, the Boeing 747s, measure 70.66 meters (232 feet) in length and carry as many as 500 passengers.

Cockpit

Galley (kitchen)

Turbofan engines

Front exit for passengers

First class

Business class

Retractable undercarriage

Weather radar in nose

QANTAS
THE AUSTRALIAN AIRLINE

Passenger seats

Passenger seats are in the upper part of the fuselage. The area below is for storage. The arrangement of the seats depends on the width of the fuselage. The seats clip onto a grid so the cabin layout can be changed easily.

 Flying Fact

Modern airliners contain the latest technical advances. Meters and dials in the cockpit instrument panel have been replaced by computer-controlled television screens.

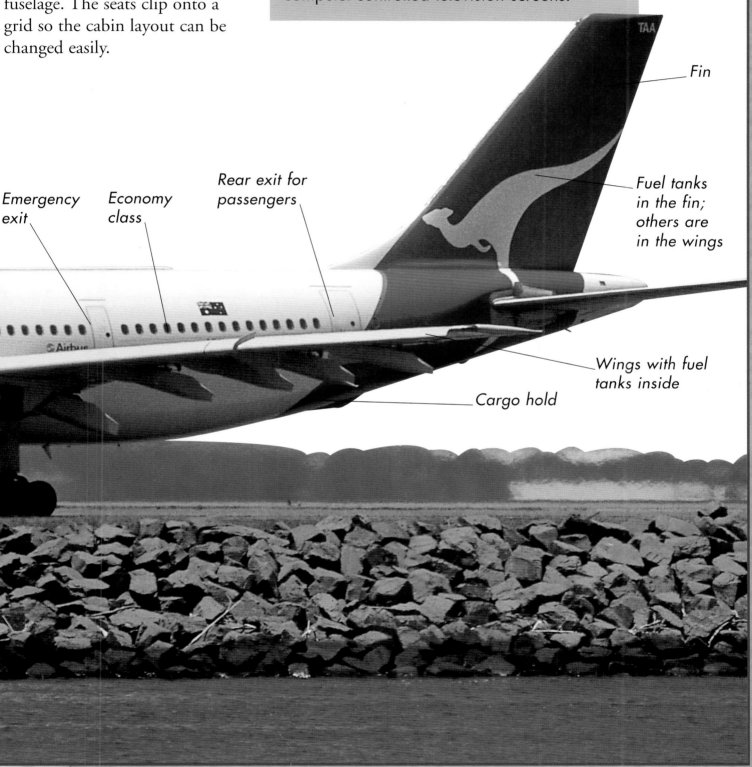

Fin

Fuel tanks in the fin; others are in the wings

Emergency exit

Economy class

Rear exit for passengers

Wings with fuel tanks inside

Cargo hold

Airports

THERE ARE AIRPORTS in most countries of the world. Every year, millions of people pass through an airport and hundreds of thousands of planes take off and land.

SUPPORT FACILITIES AND SERVICES

Airports provide support facilities and services to keep aircraft flying safely and efficiently. Extensive refuelling facilities and emergency stand-by services are needed at large airports. Customs and security arrangements are necessary for passengers.

Large international airports are like cities. They contain shops, banks, restaurants and parking facilities. An enormous work force is needed to keep airports functioning effectively. Cooks, cleaners, service staff and security officers are just some of the people needed to keep an airport working effectively and keep aircraft flying.

AIR TRAFFIC CONTROL

Pilots cannot rely on seeing other aircraft in the sky and need help to fly safely. In the area around and above an airport, each airplane is tracked by an air traffic controller. Its height and position are shown on radar screens.

Air traffic controllers speak to the captain by radio, giving instructions for a safe take-off and landing.

An air traffic controller.

When permission for take-off is granted, the airliner taxis onto the runway. When the airliner is travelling fast enough on the runway to fly (about 250 kilometers (155 miles) per hour), the captain gently pulls back the control column. The aircraft lifts its nose and climbs into the air.

Landing

When an airliner approaches the airport at the end of its flight, the captain radios air traffic control to ask permission to land. The controllers assist the crew in flying the airliner safely to the runway clear of other traffic.

The captain cuts the engine power back to make the airliner lose speed and height as it comes in to land. The raised nose of the airliner allows the main wheels to touch the ground first, which absorbs the shock of landing.

As soon as the airliner is on the ground, the captain usually puts the engines into reverse thrust and applies the wheel brakes to slow down the aircraft.

Melbourne Airport, Australia.

TAKING OFF AND LANDING

Taking off

The flight crew check that the airliner's instruments and systems are working correctly. When the airliner is ready to leave, the captain radios the control tower for permission to start the engines and taxi. The airliner waits there for permission to take off from the air traffic controllers.

Stacking

When many aircraft are waiting to land at an airport, they line up in a vertical stack while flying fixed flight patterns. They join the stack at the top level and are gradually cleared to descend to lower levels until they come out at the bottom level to make their landing approach.

Concorde

CONCORDE WAS THE world's first **supersonic** passenger aircraft. It flies at over twice the speed of sound (Mach 2). Britain and France cooperated in the design of Concorde and it first flew in 1969. Concorde was used to carry passengers from 1976.

Today, British Airways and Air France operate a small number of these airliners, offering a luxurious but expensive service to passengers between Europe and the United States. Concorde can fly passengers to their destination in little more than half the time taken by other airliners.

Flying Fact

The Concorde cruises at a height of about 17 kilometers (10.5 miles). There is much less drag on the aircraft at this height and the thrust of the engines can propel Concorde up a speed over Mach 2.

Concorde.

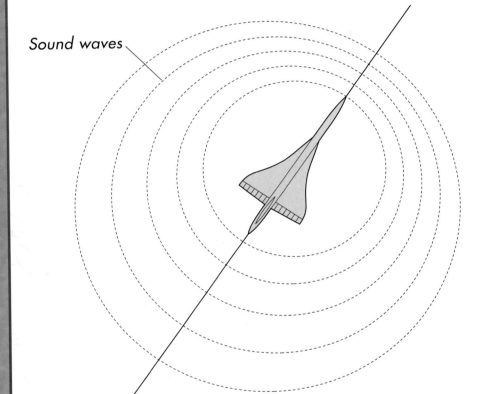

Sound waves

**Subsonic flight
(slower than sound)**
When Concorde flies slower than the speed of sound, sound waves noise from an aircraft's engine move away faster than Concorde is flying.

Flying at Mach 1
When Concorde flies at Mach 1, it moves forward at the same speed as sound waves.

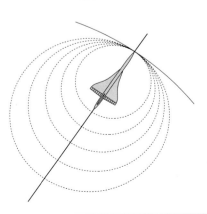

Flying at Mach 2
When Concorde flies at Mach 2, its special shape stays within the shock waves generated by the nose to prevent an increase in drag.

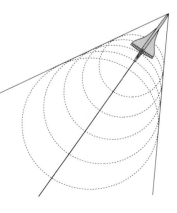

Sea planes and flying boats

Seaplanes and **flying boats** are airplanes that can take off and land on water. Flying boats are usually large aircraft, while seaplanes are smaller.

Flying boats have a hull-shaped fuselage and wing-tip floats to keep them balanced. They are sometimes used for passenger and **freight** transportation, but their main role is in fire-fighting.

Seaplanes have floats in place of the undercarriage of land-based airplanes. They are used for transportation in areas of the world where it is difficult to build runways but where there are stretches of water such as lakes for landing.

AMPHIBIANS

Amphibians are airplanes that can land on water and land. A Cessna 206 is a modern amphibian version of a light aircraft.

A seaplane uses floats to land on the water. These can be taken off and replaced with wheels if needed.

Flight timeline

1783 In France brothers Joseph and Etienne Montgolfier launch the first successful hot-air balloon.

1852 The first steam-powered airship is flown by the French engineer Henri Giffard.

1890s The German engineer Otto Lilienthal builds and flies monoplane and biplane gliders.

1903 The Wright brothers make the first powered-aircraft flight at Kitty Hawk, the United States.

1909 French pilot Louis Bleriot makes the first successful airplane flight across the English Channel.

1910 The first commercial air service is established by Count Ferdinand von Zeppelin of Germany, using airships.

1914 World War I begins. Aircraft are used on both sides.

1919 Two British pilots, John Alcock and Arthur Whitten Brown, make the first non-stop flight across the Atlantic Ocean.

1927 The US pilot Charles Lindberg flies his Spirit of St. Louis solo across the Atlantic Ocean from New York to Paris.

1930 Frank Whittle of Great Britain takes out a patent for a jet engine.

1939 The first jet aircraft, the German He178, makes its first flight.

World War II begins. Aircraft are used on both sides.

American engineer Igor Sikorsky designs the first modern helicopter.

1947 Charles 'Chuck' Yeager breaks the sound barrier in the American Bell X-1 rocket plane, the first supersonic aircraft.

1952 The world's first jet airliner, the DeHavilland Comet, enters regular passenger service in the United Kingdom.

1970 The Boeing 747 jumbo jet enters service.

1975 The supersonic Concorde, the world's fastest airliner, goes into service.

1984 The X-29, the experimental plane, flies for the first time.

1986 Dick Rutan and Jeana Yeager make the first unrefuelled round-the-world flight in the Rutan Voyager.

1989 The B-2 stealth bomber is test flown.

1999 Bernard Piccard and Brian Jones, a Swiss doctor and a British pilot, fly around the world in a hot-air balloon.

2000 and beyond New supersonic space planes may be flying around the world carrying passengers and cargo in record-breaking times.

Airships may provide regular passenger and cargo services.

The International Space Station (ISS) will be fully functional by 2004. Astronauts and scientists will commute between Earth and the ISS to live and work in space.

People may be flying between Earth and outer space as they live and work in bases on the moon and other planets.

Glossary

ailerons — control surfaces on the rear, outer surfaces of the wings, which are used to change the direction of the plane

airfoil — a special shape used for flying; the top of the wing is curved and the bottom of the wing is straight

biplane — an aircraft with two complete sets of wings, one above the other

carbon monoxide — poisonous gas

crankshaft — the shaft to which pistons are attached in a piston engine

drag — air resistance that holds an object back

elevators — controls on the tail plane that raise or lower the plane's nose

flying boat — an aircraft with a hull shaped like a boat so that it can land on water

freight — cargo such as luggage and mail

fuselage — the body of the airplane

gliders — airplanes without engines

horsepower — a measure of power

jet — an engine that works by igniting an explosive mixture of air and kerosene

lift — the force that carries a flying object upwards when it moves through the air

maneuver — controlled movement or motion

monoplane — an aircraft with only one wing on each side

rudder — a control on the tail fin that moves the nose of the airplane left or right

subsonic — below the speed of sound

supersonic — faster than the speed of sound

thrust — the force that moves an object forward

weight — the force that pulls an object down

wing-warp — a means of twisting the wings so the aircraft will turn

Index